A Mad Wet Hen
and Other Riddles

GREENWILLOW BOOKS

A Mad Wet Hen
and Other Riddles

by Joseph Low

Greenwillow
Read-alone

A Division of William Morrow & Company, Inc., New York

10 9 8 7 6 5 4 3 2 1

Library of Congress Cataloging in Publication Data
Low, Joseph (date) A mad wet hen & other riddles.
(Greenwillow read-alone books)   Summary: A collection of riddles
for beginning readers.   1.   Riddles—Juvenile literature.
[1.   Riddles]   I.   Title. PN6371.5.L6   398.6
76-44329   ISBN 0-688-80082-3   ISBN 0-688-84082-5 lib. bdg.

Why is the figure nine

like a peacock?

Without a tail, it is nothing.

Why is a cat
crossing the Sahara Desert
like Christmas Eve?

They both have sandy claws.

Why do you feed your

little pig all day long?

So he can make a hog of himself.

Why is a moody man

like a tea kettle?

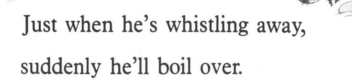

Just when he's whistling away,

suddenly he'll boil over.

What is the difference

between a fisherman

and a bad student?

One baits his hook.

The other hates his book.

What would you get
if you threw a white hen
into the Red Sea?

A mad, wet hen.

When is a boy

most like a bear?

When he is barefoot.

How is a well-dressed man
different from a warm dog?

The man wears

a complete suit.

The dog just pants.

How is an elephant different
from a flea?

An elephant can have fleas,

but a flea can't have elephants.

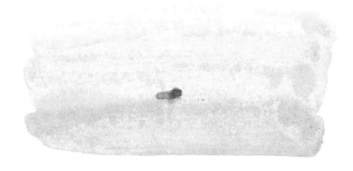

Why is a dog's tail

like the center

of a tree trunk?

It is farthest from the bark.

Who plays hard when he works,
and works hard when he plays?

A one-man band.

What is full of holes

but can still hold water?

A sponge.

What color would it make your sister
if you put a mouse in her hand?

It would make her yell, "Oh!"

What kind of ant

is the biggest ant of all?

A giant.

What flies up, but is always down?

A goose feather.

What is the difference

between a tube

and a foolish Dutchman?

One is a hollow cylinder.

The other is a silly Hollander.

Why is an ice cream cone
like a lazy donkey?

The more you lick it,

the faster it goes.

What bird looks most
like a stork?

Another stork.

What is the best thing to take
when you are run down?

The license number
of the car.

Why are umbrellas

like empty soda bottles?

They are all used up.

What does a rooster always do
when he stands on one foot?

He holds up the other one.

What is the difference
between a sigh,
a diamond
and a monkey?

A sigh is,
"Oh, dear!"

A diamond is
too dear.

And a monkey is
you, dear.

Why should you give the letter A to a deaf Egyptian princess?

·51·

It would make her hear.

What is the hardest thing
about learning to ice-skate?

The ice.

Why did my uncle Tim's mother
knit him three socks
after he had been at sea for a year?

He wrote: "I am much taller now.
I have grown another foot."